Nature's Children

WORKING ELEPHANTS

by Maggie da Silva

 Grolier Educational

FACTS IN BRIEF

Classification of the Elephant

Class:	*Mammalia* (mammals)
Order:	*Proboscidea*
Family:	*Elephantidae*
Genus and Species:	*Loxodonta africana* (African elephant); *Elephas maximus* (Asian or Indian elephant)

World distribution. In the wild in Asia and Africa; the rest of the world in captivity.

Habitat. In the wild habitats vary from damp tropical forests to grassy savannahs. Domestic animals are used, in Asia, for work in forests; in Europe and North America elephants are found mainly in zoos, preserves, and circuses.

Distinctive physical characteristics. Large size, long trunks, and tusks.

Habits. Both young and adult elephants are playful, engaging in chases and mock fighting. They also build long-term relationships with families, herds, and handlers.

Diet. Elephants are vegetarians, eating, in captivity, everything from hay to rolled oats and vegetables.

Library of Congress Cataloging-in-Publication Data

Da Silva, Maggie, 1964-
    Working elephants / Maggie da Silva.
        p.   cm. — (Nature's children)
   Includes index.
   Summary: Describes the physical characteristics, behavior,
distribution, and care of elephants.
   ISBN 0-7172-9072-7 (hardbound)
   1. Elephants—Juvenile literature.   [1. Elephants.]   I.Title.
II. Series.   97-5952
OL737.P98D3 1997   CIP
636.9'67—dc21   AC

This library reinforced edition was published in 1997 exclusively by:

 Grolier Educational

Sherman Turnpike, Danbury, Connecticut 06816

Set ISBN 0-7172-7661-9
Working Elephants ISBN 0-7172-9072-7

Contents

The mighty elephant is a gentle, intelligent, and community-minded creature. In the wild elephants work together, helping and protecting each other. In captivity they show the same kind of loyalty and affection both for each other and for their human keepers.

For centuries people have placed great value on elephants, particularly as workers. Elephants are well built for work. Some males, or bulls, can grow to be 13 feet (3.9 meters) tall and weigh more than seven tons (6.3 metric tons)—as much as a railroad car! The females, or cows, are smaller and weigh only around four tons (3.6 metric tons).

In Europe and in North and South America the only time most people get to see elephants is at a circus or zoo. But in Asia and Africa this gentle giant still lives in the wild, and in some parts of the world its work is highly important to humans. No matter what the setting, though, elephants are fascinating creatures.

In some parts of the world elephants not only work—they take people to work, too!

Creatures from the Ancient Past

Elephants have been around for millions of years, sharing our planet with both ancient creatures and humans. The elephant's earliest ancestor, the Moerithium, looked nothing like the elephants of today. It was small and had no trunk or tusks. In fact, it looked more like a pig with a large, elephantlike skull. The Moerithium roamed Egypt around 45 million years ago.

Over millions of years descendants of the Moerithium evolved into large animals with trunks and tusks. Two well-known descendants were the wooly mammoth and the somewhat smaller mastodon. By the end of the ice age these elephant ancestors were extinct, but 350 other elephant species had evolved.

Today there are only two surviving elephant species: the African elephant and the Asian elephant. They can be found in certain parts of Africa and southern Asia.

In the wild elephants are gentle and community-minded.

Asian Elephants

Asian elephants (sometimes called "Indian" elephants) are the type usually found at zoos or circuses because they are considered easier to train than their African cousins. They are slightly smaller than African elephants; the bulls are around nine feet (2.7 meters) tall and weigh about five tons (4.5 metric tons).

The Asian elephant has an arched back. Its head, which it carries low, has two large, round bumps on the front. Its skin is light gray or beige and often has pink or white spots. It has a smooth trunk and either small tusks or no tusks at all. Its ears are small and well suited to its native forest habitat, as they are less likely to catch on branches and vines.

In the wild Asian elephants live in the hilly forests of India, Sri Lanka, Southeast Asia, southern China, and the islands of Sumatra and Borneo.

Asian elephants are known for their small ears and the two round bumps on their heads.

African Elephants

African elephants are larger than Asian elephants and are divided into two types: the larger bush elephant and the smaller forest elephant. The male African bush elephant is the largest land mammal on earth.

African elephants have a dip in their backs behind their shoulders and hold their flat, sloping heads higher than Asian elephants. They are dark gray and have ringed rather than smooth trunks. They also have much larger tusks than Asians (sometimes 11 feet, or 3.3 meters, long), and their ears are at least twice as big.

The African forest elephant lives in the dense forests of the Congo River basin in central and western Africa. The larger bush elephant lives on the savannahs, or grassy plains, of central and southern Africa, south of the Sahara.

African elephants have large ears and rings on their trunks.

Elephants and People

Elephants and people have a long history together. In ancient times people hunted the animals for both their meat and their ivory tusks. Elephants have also been used for work and transportation, in religious ceremonies, and for entertainment. In war rulers such as Alexander the Great used elephants to carry soldiers and cargo, as well as to frighten the enemy.

More recently, however, wild elephants and people have had trouble living together. The growing human populations of Asia and Africa have taken over elephant feeding grounds.

With less space to graze, elephants have eaten valuable crops and angered farmers. Hungry elephants have also been known to pull down telephone poles and knock down huts in their search for food. Many Asian and African nations are attempting to solve this problem by setting up wildlife reserves (large tracts of land) where elephants can roam freely.

Humans and elephants have worked together for thousands of years.

Even in captivity elephants are a majestic sight.

Life on a Reserve

On a wildlife reserve in Africa or Asia acres and acres of the elephant's natural environment are fenced in, giving the animals a protected living area. Within the fences elephants and other wild animals can roam freely and safely, because no one is allowed to hunt animals on a reserve. Unfortunately, illegal hunters—called poachers—disobey the laws and kill protected animals anyway.

Elephant poachers risk punishment in order to obtain the valuable ivory in elephant tusks. Ivory has long been used to make some of the world's most beautiful jewelry and artwork. It also is believed to have special healing powers.

Wildlife reserves face many challenges, from poachers to lack of space. But without the efforts of the dedicated people who manage these reserves— and of the governments that try to protect the animals—there would be little chance for elephants to survive in their native habitat.

Built to Work

The elephant's powerful body makes it especially well suited for hard work. The big bones in its legs are stacked on top of one another, giving it great strength, balance, and agility. An elephant's feet are heavily padded, allowing it to walk quite daintily over the roughest terrain.

Elephants—especially working elephants—use their trunks and tusks as tools. The elephant uses its tusks for digging and sometimes for lifting and carrying.

The trunk is a unique feature. It is about six feet (1.8 meters) long, and the elephant uses it as a combination arm, nose, and ... shower hose! Forty thousand muscles and tendons make the trunk extremely strong and flexible. An elephant can use its trunk to lift large, heavy objects (up to 600 pounds, or 272 kilograms) or to perform very delicate tasks like picking up a penny.

Elephants' trunks make useful tools.

Logging Elephants

Although bulldozers and tractors do much of the logging work in Asia today, elephants are still used in terrain that is too rough for machines. In the dense forests of Asia elephants carry huge logs down mountainsides where machines cannot go. They deposit the logs into rivers to float downstream, where other elephants pull the logs out and feed them into a giant saw.

Logging elephants are rigorously trained, and they are well cared for. People love to work with elephants because they are so intelligent. Whoever first said, "An elephant never forgets," may have been referring to the animal's ability to remember how to do a variety of tasks.

The Mahout

Logging elephants in India and Asia start to learn their trade at around five years old. At that age the young elephant is paired with a mahout, or elephant trainer.

Traditionally, the job of the mahout is passed down from father to son, and the mahout is paired with his elephant for life! Today many mahouts go to an "elephant school," where they learn how to care for and train their animals. In school the mahout is taught how to feed, water, bathe, and groom his elephant. He learns about first aid, breeding, and caring for elephant calves, or babies.

Together, the mahout and his elephant learn to mount and dismount, give and take commands, and a variety of other skills. Over time the mahout builds a trusting friendship with the elephant. The mahout has to be careful not to overwork his elephant, which may injure itself trying to please him.

Mahouts command the elephants on the job.

The Circus

In the 1700s a circus was simply a display of unusual animals. In 1796 the first elephant was displayed in North America, to the delight of spectators. Although this animal performed no tricks, it was considered a great curiosity.

In 1821 an elephant named Old Bet performed the first elephant tricks. For the astounded audience, she pulled a cork from a bottle and drank the contents. She laid down, sat up, and even whistled—all on command!

By this time it was fashionable to display a menagerie, or group of different animals. Circuses often had groups of elephants that formed pyramids and did other tricks.

Elephants did more than just entertain spectators, however. They were also used to pull the heavy wagons of the circus and to lift the huge poles that held up the circus tent.

Soon elephants became merely part of the spectacle and were no longer the main attraction. It wasn't until much later that another elephant would become as famous as Old Bet.

Elephants have starred in circuses for hundreds of years.

Jumbo

In 1882 the famous circus owner, P. T. Barnum, bought a huge elephant named Jumbo from the London Zoo. When Jumbo arrived in America, he caused quite an uproar.

Jumbo weighed over six tons (5.4 metric tons) and stood at least ten feet (3 meters) high. He was billed as the "Largest Living Quadruped (four footed creature) on Earth" and became the main attraction of the Barnum & Bailey Circus. Children were anxious to ride him, and his name was attached to all kinds of products, from cigars to peanuts to hats!

In 1885 Jumbo was killed in a train accident. But to this day, over a hundred years later, Jumbo's name continues to be used to describe anything big—from jumbo shrimp to jumbo jets.

Circus Tricks

Circus elephants are quite accomplished when it comes to tricks. They can march in single file, grasping the tail of the elephant in front of them with their trunks. They can kneel and then extend a foot so keepers can mount their trunks.

People are often surprised at how nimble and balanced elephants are. They can sit up and "beg," balance on either their front or hind legs, walk on a ball, and even stand on their heads!

Circus elephants learn to do precise tasks with their trunks, such as picking up a coin, playing the harmonica, or squirting water on command. A trained elephant can delicately pick someone up with its trunk and then spin the person around!

Circus workers say that many elephants enjoy the attention they get when performing. The animals particularly like the time before and after their performances, when people line up to give them peanuts and other treats.

Circus elephants can perform astonishing tricks.

A ride on an elephant is a thrill for anyone.

The Zoo

In zoos elephants get plenty of attention and exercise. They receive daily showers from their keepers, who also trim their big toenails. A large stable and enclosure usually are provided for the animals, as well as a bathing pool and a rubbing post so they can scratch themselves. The elephants are routinely walked around the grounds, and sometimes zoo elephants give rides. Many zoos also have elephant shows, where people can see how the clever animals are trained.

In a zoo elephants have their meals carefully balanced. Captive elephants need less food than they do in the wild, but they tend to need a more nutritious diet. Zookeepers make sure the animals get what they need and that they have plenty of water at all times.

No Meat for Me, Please

Elephants are herbivores, which means they are vegetarians and eat no meat. Elephants are big eaters, though, and they will eat almost any plant. In captivity elephants are fed about 100 pounds (45 kilograms) of food each day—only a third of what they would eat in the wild. Unlike their wild counterparts zoo elephants are in danger of getting fat!

Elephants are fed hay, rolled oats, vegetables, fruit, special pellets, and occasionally, special treats like bread. Captive elephants are also given nutritional supplements to make sure they stay healthy.

Elephants drink a lot of water—up to 50 gallons (189 liters) each day. They also need salt, which is added to their food or provided on a salt lick (a big block of salt).

In zoos elephants are cleaned and scrubbed often.

Elephant Behavior

Elephants are famous for their intelligence, a quality that is evident in their ability to use tools. When an elephant has an itch on its back, for example, it will use a stick to scratch itself—just as a person would. Elephants are also known to work together to figure out problems, even how to free a comrade trapped in mud.

Elephants are also extremely brave. An elephant mother will protect her children from any enemy no matter how dangerous. Elephants can use their trunks and tusks to fight, and they will also stomp on an attacker with their feet.

Elephants are also loyal and affectionate. They build long-term relationships with each other and with special human beings. When two elephants meet, they touch trunks or rub shoulders. Sometimes they put the tips of their trunks together, as if they are kissing. Elephants like to stand very close together, caressing and patting each other. People who care for elephants will often say that they believe the animals trust and love them.

*When two elephants meet, they touch
trunks—almost as if they are kissing.*

Elephant Talk

Sound is very important to elephants. Even in the limited space of a zoo sound is the animal's main form of communication. When an elephant is excited or angry, it will let out an ear-splitting trumpet through its trunk, just as it would in the wild.

Elephants make other sounds too—barks, snorts, screams, roars, growls, and thumps. One of the more interesting signals they use is stomach rumbles. They control this noise by expanding and contracting their stomach muscles. Experts used to think the rumbles were the sound of digestion! Now they understand that the rumbles are one of the many different ways in which elephants communicate with each other.

Although elephants in captivity do not need to use sound to find food, locate each other, search for mates, or warn of danger, they continue to use sound as their favorite form of expression.

Elephants are excellent parents who take good care of their young.

Mating Habits

Elephant bulls can mate when they are 10 or 11 years old. Cows are ready to mate and have babies when they are 12, although they usually do not have their first calves until they are around 16.

Elephants can mate at any time, but wild elephants mate only about once a year. In the wild the males battle each other for the right to mate with a female.

In captivity elephants' mating habits are different. Zookeepers will usually choose an elephant's mate, and they closely monitor the animals' activities. Some zoos allow their elephants to mate naturally, but often there is simply not enough space for the mating rituals. Instead, zookeepers will use artificial insemination, which is a way of impregnating the female without the animals actually mating.

Elephants—especially mothers and babies— like to stand close together.

*Baby elephants are helped by their mothers and by
older "aunts" as well.*

The Birth Ritual

After an elephant cow becomes pregnant, she carries her baby for between 19 and 22 months— almost two years! After all that time, she gives birth to a single calf. Twins are very rare.

Elephants perform a special ritual for every baby that is born. First, one "aunt" cow helps the expectant mother pick a comfortable spot for the birth. Then, when the pregnant cow is ready, she trumpets to the other cows, who make a protective circle around her while she gives birth.

When the calf is born, the aunt separates it from the mother, as new mothers sometimes accidentally hurt their babies. When the mother is calm, the aunt returns her calf. Then the aunt and the other cows nudge and support the newborn with their trunks until it is able to stand.

In many zoos the zookeepers try to re-create this natural birth situation for pregnant cows.

Born in Captivity

An elephant birth is a big event at a zoo, and keepers will do their best to make sure it is successful. A pregnant zoo elephant is also carefully monitored to make sure she is healthy and her pregnancy is going well.

Breeding elephants in captivity is very important to the future of the species. Most zoos share what they learn with other zoos and with breeding programs in countries where wild herds of elephants are diminishing.

One fun part of a zoo birth is choosing a name for the baby! Usually, the zoo will have a contest. The keepers will then try to choose a name for the baby that will also suit it when it is a dignified, grown-up elephant.

Even on a reserve young elephants get attention from human visitors.

Growing Up

A baby elephant is small and weak—for an elephant, that is. At birth a calf is about three feet (0.9 meters) tall and weighs about 200 pounds (91 kilograms).

Whether in the wild or captivity the calf will be carefully protected by the other elephants. In a zoo the baby will play outside with its mother and aunts watching over it. In an atmosphere of care and protection the calf will grow rapidly and learn quickly about its home at the zoo.

A baby elephant drinks its mother's milk until it is about two years old. Although a newborn calf can digest solid food, it cannot chew, so the mother or aunt chews the food first and then gives it to the calf. When a calf is three or four months old, it can eat vegetables and other plant foods on its own.

Mother elephants love to shower attention on their babies. They wash them, nuzzle them with their trunks, and are always near to protect them from danger.

Grown-up elephants can do any number of different jobs for people.

Play

Young elephants love to play. They like to chase each other, push and shove, pull tails, and butt heads. As they grow older, calves like to engage in play fights. All of this helps them develop their strength and coordination.

When two elephants play fight, they charge at each other, push with their trunks, and play tug of war. Sometimes, play fights can be dangerous, but adult elephants will usually break up a fight before a calf gets hurt.

A few days after it is born, a baby elephant figures out how its trunk works. Soon its trunk becomes a favorite toy. Calves love to squirt water at themselves, other elephants—and at people. Calves also quickly learn how to blow bubbles!

Both adults and baby elephants like to play. When the calves tease or play tag with them, adults will often join in the fun. But if the play gets too rowdy, the adults will remind the calves to behave themselves.

Musth

Keeping elephants, especially in zoos and circuses, can be a challenge, especially because of a substance known as musth (pronounced must). Each year elephants— especially bulls —stain their faces with oily musth from glands located at the sides of their heads.

If it were just something that affected elephants' appearance, musth would simply be an annoyance. But musth is also linked to elephants' moods and behavior. While "in musth," as it is called, elephants become extremely nervous and ready to attack almost anything, including other elephants and even people.

Some captive elephants become so dangerously excitable that they must be kept isolated from other elephants. At times they must actually be tied or chained down for their own protection so they won't harm themselves in their fitlike moments.

The Future for Elephants

Elephants are in great danger from poachers. In Asia elephant poachers have killed most of the bigger, stronger bull elephants, leaving only the smaller, weaker bulls for breeding. This has endangered the species. Governments in Africa and Asia have begun to take steps against poachers, but thieves will go to great lengths to get the valuable ivory.

Elephants in captivity are also in danger of abuse. Circus animals sometimes suffer from poor training and excessive punishment. They may also suffer from the lack of a proper place to live, as well as underfeeding and bad travel conditions.

International wildlife projects work to pass laws that protect elephants from poaching and preserve their natural environment. Animal rights organizations strive to protect captive elephants from abuse and neglect. Although they are physically powerful, elephants need our help to ensure their safety and happiness.

Elephants can even play the ancient game of polo!

The Immortal Elephant

In stories elephants are often said to be magical, powerful, and wise. In ancient tales elephants appeared in the sky before a war, led lost children to safety, and even rescued kidnapped royalty!

Today elephants still seem to have a reputation for having magical powers. The popular cartoon Dumbo is about a big-eared elephant who learns to fly, while the famous Babar books tell about a young elephant who goes to the city and eventually is crowned king of elephant land!

Elephants are a popular symbol of strength and power. Pictures of elephants can be found on ancient Egyptian tombs and on Roman coins.

As an emblem of power and wisdom, the elephant has very little competition. No wonder so many people have been inspired to immortalize this remarkable animal!

Words to Know

Aunt   An elephant cow that assists in an elephant birth ritual.

Bull   A male elephant.

Cow   A female elephant.

Habitat   The area in which a creature lives.

Ivory   The valuable material that makes up an elephant's tusks.

Jumbo   Originally, the name of an extremely large circus elephant; now, anything large or oversized.

Mahout   An elephant trainer.

Musth   A substance that comes from glands at the side of an elephant's head.

Poacher   An illegal hunter.

Reserve   An area free of hunting that has been set aside for the preservation of wildlife.

Quadruped   A creature with four legs.

Savannah   Grassland.

Trumpet   The loud sound made through an elephant's trunk.

Trunk   The long, hoselike body part at the end of an elephant's head.

INDEX

Cover Photo: SuperStock, Inc.
Photo Credits: Robert Christian (Unicorn Stock Photos), page 35; Clark Coleman (Unicorn Stock Photos), page 7; Gerry Ellis (Gerry Ellis Nature Photography), page 8; Rod Furgason (Unicorn Stock Photos), pages 11, 31; Dede Gilman (Unicorn Stock Photos), page 33; Jeff Greenberg (Unicorn Stock Photos), page 26; Martin Harvey (The Wildlife Collection), page 20; Martin R. Jones (Unicorn Stock Photos), page 29; A. Rodham (Unicorn Stock Photos), page 41; SuperStock, Inc., pages 4, 13, 17, 22, 25, 36, 39, 44; Dennis Thompson (Unicorn Stock Photos), page 14.